This book belongs to:

____

Dedication

To my beautiful mother your strength and love built the foundation I stand on. You taught me to endure storms and pour encouragement into others with grace.
To my daughters and godchildren, you are my heartbeat. Your light fuels my purpose and inspires me to keep lifting the next generation.
To my earthly king thank you for believing in the vision God placed in me. Your support gives me strength to keep building and dreaming.
To my sandbox friends, new friends, bonus parents, siblings, and extended family your love, wisdom, and laughter anchor me through every season.
And to every child I've encouraged or held close in moments of doubt this book is for you. Every spark of confidence you've shown lives forever in these pages.
This work is my offering to all of you. May you always know you are seen, valued, and worthy.

In a world that can feel loud and unkind, one girl learned the power of believing in herself.

Patty Ann wasn't always confident she once felt small and unsure until a magical moment reminded her how strong and wonderfully made, she truly was.

Now she shares that light with others, lifting hearts and spreading hope wherever she goes.

 This is the story of how Patty Ann became the Confident Godmother one kind word at a time.

Open these pages and discover how that same magic confidence lives inside of you.

BAKERY

Once upon a time, in a small town, there lived a little girl named Patricia Ann.

She was kind and thoughtful, but she often felt sad because her clothes were not as fancy as the other children's.

At school, Patricia Ann was often teased and bullied because of her clothes.

She would come home feeling hurt and lonely, wishing she could be as confident as the other children.

Patricia Ann would sit alone during lunch and recess, pretending not to hear the mean words. She wondered if she would ever feel happy, brave, or enough.

One sunny afternoon, Patricia Ann sat beneath an old oak tree and cried.

She whispered, "I wish I could help others feel happy. But how can I when I don't even believe in myself?"

Suddenly, a soft breeze swept through the air.

Leaves swirled gently around her, and a warm, glowing light shimmered near the tree.

Out of the light stepped a ......
Beautiful...

FAIRY!

Hello, Patricia Ann," the fairy said kindly.
"I'm Lily Ann, your fairy friend. I've been watching over you, and today is your special day."

"Exactly," said Lily Ann. "You have a heart full of love, and that's more powerful than anything. I have a gift to help you see it."

Lily Ann waved her wand, And a magical mirror floated in the air.

"Look into this mirror and repeat after me.
These words are the truth of who you are."

Patricia Ann stood in front of the mirror. As she repeated each word, the mirror glowed brighter:
P – Powerful
A – Amazing
T – Talented
T – Thoughtful
Y – You Matter
A – Authentic
N – Never Give Up
N – Not Afraid to Shine

Patricia Ann stood taller. Her heart felt brighter.

The mirror vanished.

Lily Ann placed a glowing necklace with the letter "P" around her neck. "From now on, you are Patty-Ann, the Confident Godmother," Lily Ann said. "

"Her necklace glowed so brightly, shining like a star!

In that magical moment, Lily Ann revealed a vision of her future.
"You will bring courage and love to children all over the world.'"

"Patricia Ann's feet began to lift from the ground, and before she knew it, she was flying.

"In that very moment, Patricia Ann transformed into Patty Ann. She was no longer just a little girl; she was now the Confident Godmother."

With a shimmer of light,
Patty Ann's new outfit appeared: a
colorful kimono that danced in the
wind, a wide brimmed hat, blue jeans,
gym shoes and flowing hair.

Patty-Ann's first mission came quickly. She met a little girl named Chloe, crying by the swings. "They said I can't dance," Chloe sobbed.

Patty-Ann knelt beside her. "You are powerful and talented, Chloe. Let's dance together!"
Soon, Chloe was spinning and smiling, her confidence shining like the sun.

One day, she met a boy named Malik who was mean to others. "Why do you push people away?" Patty-Ann asked.
"Because I feel small," he whispered. "I want to be big and strong."

Malik's eyes shimmered with hope as he repeated the words.

He glanced up at Patty Ann and whispered, "Sometimes I feel small... but now, I think I can grow big and strong on the inside, too."

Patty Ann nodded proudly. "That's where true strength begins, Malik right in your heart."

Patty Ann smiled warmly. "Kindness," she said softly, "is the greatest strength of all. Now, say it with me I am powerful. I am thoughtful. I can be a friend."

Patty-Ann carried her bright torch of confidence wherever she went, helping children rise, shine, and believe in themselves. Every smile she sparked, every heart she lifted, made her light grow even stronger. And now that light lives in you, too. Always remember... you are Powerful, Amazing, Talented, Thoughtful, You Matter, Authentic, Never Give Up, and Not Afraid to Shine. The world truly needs your light.

The End....

— Patty Ann

"Your
imagination
is your
future self.

– Patty Ann

"Confidence is your imagination crown.
"Stand tall wear it well.

– Patty Ann

"Step forward feet are made to walk forward."

– Patty Ann

"Your sparkle is a snowflake one of a kind."

– Patty Ann

"Shine bright, little one
the world needs your
glow."

– Patty Ann

"Confidence doesn't mean you're never scared it means you show up anyway."

— Patty Ann

"Every step forward counts. Make every move count.

"Shine bright, because
the world needs your
light.

– Patty Ann

"Bravery isn't loud
sometimes it whispers,
'Try one more time.'"

— Patty Ann

PATTY ANN LEGACY
I AM PATTY ANN
SKYLAR'S FIRST DAY OF SCHOOL
BAKERY
SCHOOL
COMING SOON
By Patty Ann

I AM PATTY ANN

NEVER GIVE UP!

COMING SOON

By *Patty Ann*

I AM PATTY ANN
YOU CAN DO IT!
PATTY ANN LEGACY
COMING SOON
By Patty Ann

I AM PATTY ANN
MADISON STAND STRONG
PATTY ANN LEGACY
HIGH SCHOOL
COMING SOON
By Patty Ann

I AM PATTY ANN
THE POWER OF BEING YOU
MIDDLE SCHOOL
COMING SOON
By Patty Ann
PATTY ANN LEGACY